# BUSINESS TRUISMS

**Tips for Avoiding Self-Destruction on the Job**

## VINCENT TOROSCATA

iUniverse, Inc.
New York   Bloomington

**Business Truisms**
**Tips for Avoiding Self-Destruction on the Job**

*iUniverse books may be ordered through booksellers or by contacting:*

*iUniverse
1663 Liberty Drive
Bloomington, IN 47403
www.iuniverse.com
1-800-Authors (1-800-288-4677)*

*Because of the dynamic nature of the Internet, any Web addresses or
links contained in this book may have changed since publication and may
no longer be valid. The views expressed in this work are solely those of
the author and do not necessarily reflect the views of the publisher, and
the publisher hereby disclaims any responsibility for them.*

*ISBN: 978-1-4502-2631-8 (sc)
ISBN: 978-1-4502-2632-5 (ebook)*

*Printed in the United States of America*

*iUniverse rev. date: 04/28/2010*

*To my friend, Ignatius DiPasquale. You left us before you could see your work published. So, Iggy, this is for you.*

# Contents

# Introduction

I began writing this book in 2007 after my friend Iggy passed away. We had always talked about publishing our stuff, but we never got around to doing it. Iggy had penned a whole bunch of essays and musings, and he promised that he would let me edit his work and prepare it to be submitted to a publisher. That never happened, so I embarked upon this mission: to write a book to fulfill a wish that Iggy and I had discussed in numerous phone calls.

This book is a compilation of my ideas and theories about things that happen in the office. The ideas are the result of my experiences at each of my Wall Street employers. They are based further on conversations I've had over the years with co-workers, commuter pals, and acquaintances. We would trade war stories, triumphs as well as defeats, and we would compare notes. I have no proof that what I theorized actually happened as I described it, or whether or not it happens today.

I cannot prove the validity of the things I describe in this book, but I do believe that what I describe here happens in companies all over America, if not the world. People, for the most part, react the way that I describe, or have noticed others reacting this way. So, read on, form your own opinion, and decide for yourself if what I describe here happens at your place of business.

I've listed the truisms in no particular order, or I should say, they are listed in the order in which I came up with them. I chose not to change the order just for the sake of making the ideas flow more smoothly. I developed the ideas expressed in the book in this order, and I want to share them with you in the same order.

At the time that I started writing this book, I worked on Wall Street. By the time I sent the manuscript to the publisher, I no longer worked for the same company. I chose not to make any changes to what I'd written to account for the change in my circumstances. When I write about "my employer," the reference is to my employer at the time that I was writing the book, or to my previous employer on Wall Street. In some cases, I have simply reworked and reworded situations that were relayed to me by others. Whether I actually participated in the situations I describe is not the issue. What I describe in these pages did happen, may happen, or could happen to people in different circumstances in offices all around the country and the world. I have come to this conclusion based on my conversations with others, and based on my own experiences.

I share these experiences with you. Learn from them. Use these tips to avoid self-destructing on the job.

# CHAPTER 1

# Anonymous Communication

*No communication, electronic or otherwise, is ever truly anonymous.*

Do you have a facility at work that permits you to post suggestions or complaints anonymously online? It generally works along the following lines. Log on to the corporate Web site. Go to the "suggestion box" page (or whatever the company calls it), select an appropriate topic, and type your suggestion or complaint. The idea is that you can say what you want to say without fear of reprisal.

Can you say "electronic signature"? Are you familiar with keystroke-logging software? I don't know whether or not my employer uses a "key logger," but I do believe that every electronically submitted communication can be traced back to its origins. When your employer tries to convince you that you can submit your suggestion or complaint anonymously, you should realize that you can be found out if management really wants to know. Also, consider that you can just as easily type out your suggestion and mail it to a post office box. It's a lot tougher to trace something that is "snail mailed," but the company will strongly recommend that you use the new electronic suggestion box in the interest of saving time. Perhaps it is easier and less expensive to process electronic communications, but it is easier and less expensive for the company, not necessarily for you, especially if you factor in the cost of being found out.

Ask yourself this: If the company is sincerely interested in hearing what I have to say, why does it provide a way of communicating anonymously? When you speak to someone, don't you want to know that person? I'm not talking about idle chatter or casual conversation. When you engage in an exchange of ideas, don't you want to be able to relate to the person who is speaking (or in the case of the suggestion box, the person who is writing)? Anonymity doesn't seem to fit here. It seems counterintuitive. You would want to know who is making the suggestion.

The company knows that you are reluctant to express your true feelings out of fear of reprisal. If you are only offering a suggestion or a recommendation, why should there be any fear of reprisal? Does it make sense to ask someone to express an opinion, and then punish the person because you don't like what he or she said? It seems to me that what the company is really saying is that it wants to hear what you have to say, but reserves for itself the right to chastise you if it doesn't agree with your opinion. While you are thinking about that, give some consideration to the person who reads what is submitted to the electronic suggestion box. Do you know how many people are reading what you've submitted? Who is ever going to find out that you were the one who made the suggestion, if it's a good one?

The company controls the electronic suggestion box. Once you make a submission, it's out of your control. The means exist to trace the communication back to its source. Snail mail may take a little longer to get to its destination, but it's easier for the sender to avoid detection. Unless someone is watching your every move, following you to the post office, and retrieving your anonymous suggestion (interfering with postal delivery is a federal offense the last time I checked), there is less chance you will be chastised, because there is less chance you will be found out.

Still, the odds of being identified aren't entirely eliminated when you use snail mail. You always run the risk of being discovered whenever you put pen to paper, literally or figuratively. If you really believe in what you have to say, and are willing to defend your position, even to the point of risking dismissal, go ahead and send in your suggestion or complaint. If you worry about the consequences and are afraid of reprisals, keep your opinion to yourself; don't fall into the trap of believing that the company is really interested in what you have to say. If management were really interested in what you had to say, you'd be a member of the management team on some level.

# CHAPTER 2

*m*

# Your Manager

---

*Your manager is not your friend.*

---

A manager manages. Manages what? A manager manages time, people, and assets, just to name a few things. A manager has to manage all of these things together, often in a seemingly contradictory fashion. The manager is charged with carrying out the directives of a more senior manager.

Most managers recognize the need to put personal feelings aside in order to get the job done. They may have to make demands of the staff. In some instances, those demands may get some people really upset; that is irrelevant. The manager is not trying to win a popularity contest. He or she is trying to win accolades from the boss, which should lead to a good performance evaluation, and, ultimately, to a wage increase or a promotion.

A manager may realize that some of the stated goals and aspirations of his or her superiors are fruitless and, perhaps, destined to fail. It doesn't matter. The only thing that counts is that these are the stated goals for the department/division/

company. The manager may express privately (as privately as a group setting will permit) that what senior management is asking (requiring) may not make sense, but it must be done. The justification for doing it is that senior management wants it done. The manager may agree with you, but he or she is toeing the party line.

So which is it? If the manager agrees with you, but still engages in the apparently fruitless pursuit, is he or she being two-faced? Or is the manager simply trying to survive, to make the best of a bad situation? And if you persist in your objections, what does that do for the manager? It makes the manager's job just a wee bit more onerous—he or she now has to manage an argumentative employee.

What do you think the manager will do? Think survival. Think about the manager's objective: garnering kudos, money, and position within the organization. If the manager lets you know that's what he or she is doing, that's OK. If the manager continues to try to make you think that he/she is on your side, think again. The manager has to survive, as do all the employees. The manager has a job to do, and you aren't making the job any easier. The manager will explain the logic (or the illogic) behind senior management's decision, but that doesn't negate the necessity of doing what senior management wants, if only because senior management wants it. The manager is being pragmatic, knowing full well that logic doesn't drive the organization. What must be done must be done.

Your friends may tell you what you want to hear. Rare is the friend who will be brutally honest with you, for many times brutal honesty will destroy a friendship. The manager is being brutally honest with you when he/she tells you that senior management wants this or that done, and that is the reason why it must be done. If you choose not to comply, you run the risk of being fired. That is brutal honesty. Your manager may like you, but he or she will fire you without hesitation if necessity dictates that it be done, or if you stand in the way of the manager fulfilling his/her duties as a manager.

# CHAPTER 3

*m*

# Your Friend, the Manager

---

*If your friend becomes a manager, see chapter 2.*

---

When you are digging ditches along with the rest of the crew, it seems only natural to bond a little with the other ditch diggers. But what happens when one of the diggers becomes a managing digger? The managing digger now assumes the responsibility for managing the ditch diggers he'd been bonding with only days/weeks/months ago. As a managing digger, he has now become one of "them," inhabitants of the dark side, purveyors of the gloom of overtime, extra work, more to do, and less time to do it. Allegiances are called into question. After all, he is/was my friend, and now he's taking "their" side. Consider, too, all the things you discussed with your friend before he became a manager. He knows how you really feel.

Your one-time friend who is now a manager has the dubious distinction of trying to make you do what the two of you once thought was an exercise in futility. Your friend must now be brutally honest with you regarding the quality of your work and the quantity of your output. Once again, you have to think survival. Your one-time friend, if he chooses to survive in his new environment, must choose between personal allegiance and monetary benefit. Unless you're paying his mortgage and putting food on his table, guess what your one-time friend will choose?

As an aside, consider this possible tactic. If you and the other ditch diggers are so tight as to present to senior management a formidable obstacle to achieving the stated goals, one or more of you may be promoted or may receive an upgrade. Those who received the upgrade or the promotion have a change of focus and a new reference group that doesn't include you. Now what do you do? If either of you becomes a manager, or if one of you receives an upgrade that puts that person in contention for becoming the other's manager, proceed with caution. Management is attempting to divide and conquer. How you deal with this situation will determine the effectiveness of this ploy.

# Chapter 4

# Hold Your Tongue

---

*Candor in a public forum is a sure means to early termination.*

---

Have you ever attended a staff meeting where the head honcho gave his rah-rah speech and then asked if anyone had questions or comments? If you ever feel the urge to stand up and say something, don't! After you've attended a few of these meetings, you will realize that although the guy giving the talk asks for input, he doesn't expect anyone to say anything, and he doesn't want anyone to say anything. He has just finished telling you what he wants you to do. He's not looking for anyone to question his logic or authority, and he certainly is not looking for anyone to argue with him. All that "this is an open forum and anyone can feel free to say anything" stuff is just window dressing.

The guy standing at the podium has been telling you what his game plan is—at least to the extent that he wants you to know it. He is senior management; you are staff. Staff follows senior management, not the other way around. So unless you're going to lay it on really thick by telling him you think he has excellent ideas (and in the process come off sounding like a real suck-up), a public forum is not the place to tell the boss what's on your mind. That the rest of the staff may agree with you is irrelevant. They are not going with you to the unemployment office. They will simply watch nonchalantly as you are escorted out the door.

I'm not saying that every public forum is set up as a "gotcha" for anyone who offers an opinion. I'm saying that the public forum is not the place to let everyone how you feel, especially if how you feel is really pissed off at management. You may believe that the policy being discussed is half-assed window dressing for the regulators; you may be upset that it will create more busy work for the staff. Now is not the time to air those feelings.

When the CEO, for example, asks if anyone has any questions, what he's really saying is "I hope no one has any questions." What if you do have a question? What if you really want to express an opinion, and you are one of those rare individuals who is adept at articulating a position in a diplomatic fashion? Should you say anything? If you openly express your opinion, however diplomatically you say it, and you happen to be right, or at the very least, you have a majority of the attendees agreeing with you, think about what that does for the person at the microphone. You've scored brownie points with your co-workers, and in the process you have embarrassed the CEO. This is not a good career move.

I associate candor with dissatisfaction. Being brutally honest in a public forum is generally combative. The speaker is telling the audience something that they may not want to hear. Brutal honesty in a situation is not usually associated with good news being announced. One would not expect there to be dissenting opinions when there's a positive development being showcased.

It is my belief that when senior management calls a general staff meeting, it's to tell you what you've already learned through the grapevine; management is formally putting its imprimatur on it. The "news" that management shares with the staff at a general meeting typically has already been discussed among the staff, in one-on-ones or in a group tête-à-tête.

So, the public forum of a general staff meeting is not the place or the time to tell senior management that you don't think that the game plan is a good one. It may make you the focus of attention for those fleeting moments when a dead silence permeates the room, and the CEO hesitates briefly before telling you, "I see your point, but ...." He may actually be saying, "Your days are numbered."

# CHAPTER 5

Your Co-workers

*Co-workers who are friendly aren't necessarily your friends.*

I've discovered that there's a big difference between being a friend and being friendly. I've made the mistake several times of thinking that someone who was friendly toward me was being my friend. I guess that some people try to be diplomatic. In trying to be diplomatic, you may invite, without realizing it, the other person to be your friend when you really can't stand that person. You don't have the heart to tell the other person to get lost, so you continue to entertain that person with what he perceives as friendship overtures.

Now, what does this do? It puts you in a position of having to listen politely to whatever this person shares with you. Believing you to be a friend, this person has entrusted to you some personal information. Since you are not this person's friend, you don't feel any obligation to keep his personal information strictly private and you proceed to share the information selectively with a few of your "friends." The process continues in this manner. The people you told tell their friends, and so on and so forth.

In one scenario, you are the recipient of the information from the person who perceives you as a friend. In another scenario, you may unknowingly impose yourself on someone whom you perceive to be a friend. As I will discuss later in another chapter, you have to distinguish between trust and friendship, both of which can be liabilities under certain circumstances. For our purposes in this chapter, the focus is on friends and friendship.

Where am I going with this? For me, at least, the concept of "friend" has a distinct connotation. If we are friends, we share information about ourselves. To the extent that we seek advice about something, we may have to tell the other person some bit of personal information about ourselves, and we expect that the information will not be discussed with anyone else. To have friendship, you have to have trust. Think about the answers to the following questions: Do you trust all the people at work with whom you are friendly? Are you friendly with all of the people you trust? Are you friendly with anyone you don't trust? Do you trust anyone you don't like, or anyone you don't consider a friend?

Be careful of what you say to people, especially if you don't trust them. Even if you do trust them, choose your words carefully. If a person is your friend, there shouldn't be any problem. It's only when you learn that your friends weren't really your friends that you may start to distrust. This distrust could end up sabotaging your career objectives, if those objectives include surviving in your current position in the company. The reality of the situation requires each of us to act as a friend one time and just friendly another time; we may even need to be apathetic, if apathy is ever an appropriate response. As long as we recognize the difference between being a friend and being friendly, and act accordingly, we will survive.

# CHAPTER 6

# Confidentiality in the Workplace

> *If you tell someone something, don't expect
> that person to keep it confidential. If it were
> truly confidential, you wouldn't have told
> anyone.*

I sit on the outskirts of civilization when it comes to office gossip and the grapevine. I'm the last person to hear anything about anyone. When I think that I've heard something that no one else knows, and I share the information with a co-worker, I find out that everyone else knew long before I was told. When someone shares allegedly confidential information with me, that person will tell me not to repeat it to anyone. Hell, everyone already knows about it, so, telling me not to tell anyone is really a joke.

I've come to the conclusion that whenever anyone shares a tidbit of information with me, and then tells me not to repeat what I've just been told, that's a signal that the information is already making its way throughout the organization or the department. It's rare that I hear something that is truly confidential, that is, something that no one else knows and that has come directly from the source, from the person to whom the information pertains. If it ever happens, it's in the context of a friend sharing a confidence, as friends often do, and I do not repeat the information to anyone, not even to my spouse. Sometimes in those circumstances, the friend is sharing the confidence for therapeutic purposes, to lighten a burden, or to elicit objective feedback. That conveyance of trust is a clear signal that the information is to be kept confidential.

Office gossip is just that: gossip. It's information that someone picked up along the way, a piece of a conversation. It is derived from assumptions and inferences based on observations, real or imagined, over a period of time. I've been the recipient of allegedly valid information about something that was about to happen, only to learn that the person who told me made assumptions based on what he'd overheard; he just guessed about the parts he did not hear.

When you tell someone something that you are planning, or when someone tells you something that he is planning (for example, getting a job at another company, or requesting a transfer, or being considered for a position in another department), we assume that information will be kept confidential. I guess that there's that feeling of belonging or wanting to belong that prompts us to tell things to people, thinking that once they know this about us, we'll be pals.

Without even thinking about what we've said, we don't think about how much of our conversation will get circulated among others inside or outside the organization. It's only when the information that we've shared gets back to us through a completely different source that we question the integrity of the person or persons to whom we've spoken. Keep in mind that at no time did anyone ever say, "Don't worry, I won't tell anyone"; or "Whatever you do, don't say anything to anyone."

The assumption (or inference, depending on your perspective) is that what we were saying or what we were being told would not be repeated.

Some people share allegedly confidential information, and then say, "Don't say anything to anyone," knowing full well that "Don't say anything to anyone" really means "Go ahead and broadcast this to the world." Once we possess the allegedly confidential information, we feel empowered. We have something that no one else has, and we know something that no one else knows. Unless others know that we know what they don't, how will others know that we are empowered and they aren't? This means that we have to let people know that we know what they don't, but once that happens, our power is lessened somewhat. Hence, the admonition, "Don't say anything to anyone." We've just empowered that person, and that person now feels compelled to let others know that he knows what they don't. The process continues in this manner until the allegedly confidential information becomes common knowledge. By that time, it becomes "Did you hear about ..." instead of "Don't say anything to anyone."

Unless the confidence is shared within the context of friendship—real friendship as opposed to the superficial relationships that sometimes pass for office friendship, don't expect the person to whom you are speaking to keep it to himself. By the same token, if you do want the word to be spread, a good way of spreading it, aside from making a public announcement, is to cloak it in the veil of confidence, leak it to the person most in need of empowerment, and count on that person to spread the word on your behalf.

# CHAPTER 7

# Shared Goals?

*What's important to you is totally irrelevant to
anyone else in the organization.*

We all have our own personal goals and aspirations. It should
not come as a surprise that one or more co-workers may not
share our enthusiasm for whatever it is that we are pursuing,
but it does. Where I am at this stage in my career bears no
relationship to anyone else's career milestone, except that we
may be next to each other on the time line, with some distance
between us depending on our respective ages.

Personal goals aside, in our jobs, we have certain duties that we
must perform. Sometimes we have to enlist the help of others
in order to complete the assigned tasks. What if the other
person has something else to do, something that has priority
over our request, at least, in his mind? I mean, doesn't he see
that I have this job to do, and these tasks to complete, and that
I need his help? Why won't he cooperate with me?

The fact is that we survive in the organization on different
levels. We're part of a group, the same department or division,

charged with accomplishing the same or similar tasks, and contributing to the same department or division goals. On that level our aspirations are the same. Our personal perspectives may be different. We may want to contribute to the common effort only to the extent that we benefit, only if it helps us achieve our personal goals. We may want the company's/department's/division's goals to be aligned with ours.

I have deadlines. There are meetings, phone calls, memos, and reports. These things are important to me in my work. I have to get them done. Do you care? You care, once again, to the extent that what I do impacts what you do. Strictly speaking, since we work for the same organization, everything that we do on the job impacts everyone else in the company; therefore, everyone in the company should care about what I do. It doesn't work that way because each of us is motivated differently, for different reasons, and in different directions.

What it comes down to is this. The guy at the top has his agenda, which we will discuss in the next chapter. His direct reports are given their marching orders; and that means that the top guy's agenda is their agenda, more or less. The direct reports now have one or more goals; and the direct reports now bark their orders to the managers and to the staff. At this level, if someone hasn't rocked the boat by questioning management's logic, the goals of the guy at the top have now become the goals of the staff, or so the theory goes. Those goals may interfere with what you have planned, or with what you think you planned. You may have had personal plans, like leaving early for a club meeting, or you may have had work plans, like putting in the overtime (gasp!) to complete a project for your manager. Even when the manager is the one causing the interference, it's just too bad. You have to deal with it.

It works the same way with co-workers, and it's particularly annoying when the co-worker is neither a person to whom you report nor someone who reports to you. It's strictly a matter of whether or not each of you has a mutually attractive goal, a goal that makes each of you want to do something to help the other person, altruism aside. If that common goal doesn't exist, there's nothing you can offer to get the other person to do what you want him to do. For each person in the organization, however, there is the ever-present, mutually attractive, and oh-so-enticing goal of survival. If we need each other in order to survive, we help each other from time to time to the extent that it contributes to our mutual survival. In that sense, what's important to him is important to me. His survival impacts my survival. His goal is my goal; and what's important to him is no longer irrelevant. It works both ways. If your survival does not have a direct impact on my survival, it's not likely that you can entice me to help you.

# CHAPTER 8

# What's in It for Me?

*Everyone has an agenda.*

Everyone has a plan. We have an idea of where we want to go and how we want to get there. Everything that we do is done with a view toward that goal. If we have a financial plan, and we're serious about that plan, we don't let anything get in the way. We find ourselves planning our social lives around the financial plan. We decide that a particular restaurant is too expensive. What we really mean is that if we go to the restaurant, we may jeopardize our financial plan.

It's the same with business plans. I'm not talking about corporate business plans, although they, too, can be considered in this discussion. Each of us has an idea of what it means to be successful; if we're serious about being successful in business, we don't let anything get in the way. If an opportunity presents itself, an opportunity to move up, or to be more successful, we'll take advantage of that opportunity. This is nothing new. We've all done it. We all do it.

The next time a co-worker suggests a course of action that

would theoretically benefit both of you, ask yourself why the co-worker is suggesting that you participate. Remember what I said earlier about altruism. What is the co-worker really trying to accomplish? Why do you have to be involved? The answer is that this person has a plan, and he needs you to help him with his plan. What better way to elicit your involvement than to show you how you can benefit—the "What's in it for me"? phenomenon.

Now, this doesn't necessarily mean that there's something wrong, or that this person has some illicit task in mind. It simply means that your goals are not his goals, and his goals are not my goals. Each of us may derive some benefit from being involved, but don't kid yourself into thinking that it's the same benefit for all of us. There's a fine line that we have to walk between being selfless and being stupid. If you frequently help others in the office with special projects, while these people rarely if ever extend a hand to help you, you have crossed over from being selfless to being taken advantage of. Don't let it happen!

Here's another perspective on the subject. Someone in the company offers you an opportunity, any opportunity. You are sold on the opportunity because of the benefit you expect to derive from getting involved, but there is still a chance you may not see this benefit. If you don't get the benefit you expected, does that mean that the person who offered you the opportunity also has not received any benefit?

If your involvement in this opportunity is needed in order for the other person to benefit, whether or not you realize any benefit, you are simply a means to an end in this person's agenda. With corporate agendas, it's difficult to separate what's in it for you from what's in it for them, because we've become co-dependent with our co-workers on company benefits, not just the medical/retirement kind. If the division does well, we all benefit, or so we're told. By the way, if you don't go along with the game plan, the company can always find someone else who's willing to participate for less pay. The division manager knows this, as he has probably been told by the senior company executives. They, in turn, have been told by the CEO that this is how it's going to be.

Once you realize that everyone has an agenda, your tactic should be to decide whether you want to go along for the ride just to see what happens, or if you really want to get involved and become an active participant. If you're just going along for the ride, you can presumably jump off any time you choose. If you're actively involved, this other person's agenda, or the company's agenda, is your agenda.

Don't ever forget that you have your own agenda, and that you should be thinking about how you can get others to help you realize your goals, whether or not there is any benefit for them. If your agenda is just to make it to retirement, you have to figure out how to get all the other players to go along. As with most things in life, that boils down to deciding how far you're willing to go in facilitating all these other agendas in order to facilitate your own.

# CHAPTER 9

# Rumors

*When a member of senior management tells you, "There's no truth to the rumor that ...," what he or she is really telling you is that he/she hasn't been told yet. It could still be true.*

There have been several meetings involving different members of senior management, some participating in the same meeting, and some hosting separate meetings with the staff. Someone inevitably asks about something that the staff is expecting to happen, or something that is rumored to be happening. The answer is typically something like, "At this time, there are no plans to ...." And that's exactly what it means. At the time that the question is asked, the subject matter is just a rumor. Five minutes after the meeting adjourns, it could become a real occurrence.

It is insulting to tell a group of employees that what they're hearing isn't true (at that particular moment in time) when you know damn well that something is in the works, or that something is being discussed, that may ultimately lead to the topic about which people are asking. Even more insulting is to send a member of senior management to the podium, someone who isn't involved in the planning, and have that person tell the staff, "There's no truth to the rumor that …," or to have that person tell the staff, "Nothing has been discussed as of today," or, "I haven't heard anything about …." The thing to remember is that the person at the podium may not know anything about the subject being discussed, or may not be involved in the negotiations about it.

Listen carefully to the question that is being asked, and listen even more carefully to the answer that is given. Pay attention, especially if the person at the podium is a lawyer, or has a law degree. A lawyer won't lie; however, a lawyer will never answer a question that hasn't been asked. The person at the podium may very well give an answer that is not responsive to the question. If the person asking the question doesn't realize that and walks away thinking that the question was answered, can you really blame the person at the podium?

When management is faced with a bunch of questions it does not want to answer yet, the tactic seems to be to give a series of non-responsive answers with the expectation that the staff eventually will get tired of asking questions and getting non-responsive answers. Sometimes the message being conveyed lies in the non-responsiveness of the answers. That is, the message being conveyed lies in what is not being said rather than what is being said. Not responding, or giving a non-responsive answer, can be a very powerful way of delivering bad news.

Occasionally, senior management may trip, even stumble badly, and fall. This usually happens when the person at the podium is conveying the party line to the staff about some particularly unpopular item (unpopular with the staff, but not necessarily with management), and the audience is not letting the manager proceed to the next topic on the agenda.

The audience keeps hammering away at the details of the message being conveyed. When this happens, the person at the podium will usually say something like, "Look, all of you were told about this weeks ago, so it should come as no surprise"; or "This was decided at the board level"; or, "It was easier for us to figure it out this way rather than the way you are suggesting." While these statements may not have been made specifically by any member of senior management, this last statement (paraphrased) was what the person at the podium said in response to a question about a particular employee benefit.

You'll see or hear this phenomenon more often in situations involving mergers, layoffs, and generally bad news at the company. In those situations, people become self-centered (the survival instinct), and want to know what alternatives are available in the event that the unthinkable (losing one's source of income) becomes thinkable. By not committing to a course of action, management cannot be held accountable if something doesn't happen the way that *you thought that management said it would happen.*

Did management really answer your question? Of course, you'll be told that management does not want to comment on what might happen (speculation) because of the tendency to treat management's speculation as fact. This is a valid concern. However, if someone asks a question, and you may not have the facts but you are certainly in a position to be able to speculate fairly and accurately as to what might happen, what's wrong with sharing that with the staff, particularly when history has shown that the speculation did ultimately become fact?

# CHAPTER 10

# Rules

---

*There is no one "set of rules." Depending on
your position in the organization, the rules
that apply to you do not apply to anyone else.*

---

Did you ever wonder why, from your point of view, other
people always seem to get away with everything? They never
seem to get caught. Yet, when you try to "squeak by" with
something minimal, you get caught. Why is that? Maybe it's
because you think that others are getting away with murder
(figuratively), but they aren't. They are playing by a different
set of rules. They are bound by a pact that is different from the
one that binds you to the organization.

You agreed to a set of work rules, a work environment, and a
salary. Your co-workers, the ones you seem to envy, have also
agreed to a set of rules, an environment, and a salary, but those
agreements are not the same as yours. You bargained one-
on-one with the organization, through a manager, to do that
which you have been assigned in return for a wage and some
benefits. The others also bargained with the organization, but
what they negotiated isn't what you negotiated. You got what

you wanted, for the most part, and so did they. That you didn't get what they got is irrelevant; it is not part of the contract.

If you want what they have, you have to bargain as they have bargained. You have to give the same "quid" that they gave in order to get the same "quo" that they received. Think of that story from the Bible about the owner of the vineyard who hired some workers in the morning, and some more workers in the afternoon, and still others later in the day. They all agreed to work for the same wage. That some worked longer than others and received the same wage has nothing to do with anything. Each worker bargained with the owner of the vineyard, and received exactly what was agreed.

In the modern organization the same principle applies, to a degree. You have no assurance that any proration will be maintained among the staff. That someone who started working at the company in July 2006 received the same bonus as someone who started working at the company in June 1979 is perfectly acceptable. Whether or not it is fair is a different issue. You can't negotiate fairness. Your agreement with the company is what it is.

That someone else negotiated something different and, perhaps, more lucrative, does not diminish the value of your contract. Think if it this way: If you had come along now instead of in 1969, you might have received the same offer that John received. The fact is that you joined the company almost forty years ago, and compared to what you were receiving forty years ago, you've come a long way. It is now time for someone else to stand in the spotlight.

If you've managed to negotiate a position for yourself in the organization that affords you some flexibility, you are one of the fortunate ones. You have some room to maneuver.

You can bargain, cajole, maneuver, and schmooze a little in order to get what you want. Add that to a mix of knowledge and determination, and you probably have a good recipe for success. Knowledge and determination alone don't make such a good batter for baking a decent career. (How's that for mixing metaphors?) The rules that once made knowledge and determination key components of a successful career have changed. It seems that who you know matters as much as, if not more than, what you know.

At my level of the organization, at this point in time, knowledge and determination don't matter much. Doing the job that has been assigned, and doing it well, isn't good enough. Oh, it's enough to get me a "satisfactory" evaluation and an unremarkable merit increase, barely keeping pace with inflation, but, it's not enough to move forward and/or upward. At my level of the organization the rules have changed, as they have changed for those just joining the organization, and as they have changed for those higher up in the organization. But the rules aren't the same for everyone. It appears that each employee is held to a different standard, without regard to rank or length of service.

This is all common sense. There's no major discovery here, no significant pronouncement of what was or what is to come. What is particularly irksome is the way in which this attitude pervades the organization. It seems that everyone knows it, but that there is no way to work around it. You just have to deal with it, not necessarily become part of it.

You have to play by the rules in order to survive in the organization. But if the rules are different for each person, at each level, and across the same level, what rules do you follow? How do you play the game? You play the game by guessing the rules that have to be followed (hopefully, guessing correctly), and then doing what has to be done in order to move forward/upward. If you don't know the rules, you must learn them from someone who has played and won (moved forward/upward), or learn them from someone who has played and lost (moved laterally/downward). If you choose not to play by the rules, you become a pariah (for playing by a different set of rules), or you become an afterthought (for not playing at all).

# CHAPTER 11

## Big Brother

---

*There's always someone watching/listening.*

---

A very long time ago, when I used to believe that you attended office parties in order to socialize and have fun, I attended an office party, and I was enjoying myself. There was food, and I ate. There was alcohol, and I drank. People were laughing and joking, and I laughed and joked. I found out later, maybe the next day, that my supervisor and his boss were watching me. My supervisor politely advised me that my actions at the office party did not make a good impression. I thought, "What actions? I was eating and drinking along with everyone else." I didn't think that I ate any more than anyone else at the party. I didn't think that I drank any more than anyone else at the party.

I learned that you attended an office party to be seen, not to eat, drink, or socialize. It appeared that I committed a cardinal sin by actually getting involved in a social gathering with my co-workers. At the following year's office party, I simply approached the food table and took small portions, grabbed a cup of soda, and sat off to the side. There was no joking around, and not too much laughing on my part. Either it made a good impression, or it made no impression, since the next day no one said anything to me about my actions at the party. Needless to say, I didn't attend any more office parties after that last episode.

You have to be careful in the office when you're talking to someone. You have to be aware of who is in the general vicinity, who is within earshot, or who is actually listening to your conversation, aside from the person to whom you are speaking. In an office with cubicles, you can be talking to the person across from you, and the people on either side of you are listening to the conversation. Most of the time it's hard to avoid because of the acoustics.

To deal with this dilemma, some people talk in small groups, and in a low tone, so that the only way to eavesdrop is to become part of the group. The situation has gotten to the point where even to be seen talking in a small group suggests that you may be trying to hide something, as a senior executive once suggested, jokingly but seriously, when she passed by a group of us who were engaged in an animated but muted conversation that stopped when she passed by.

If you make an effort to mute the conversation, either by whispering or by closing the door, if you're fortunate enough to have an office, anyone watching may interpret that as your attempt to hide something. Maybe you are, and maybe you have a valid reason, but to the person who is watching, it looks suspicious. Forget that the person who is watching may have no business watching you or anyone else in the office. The fact is that someone saw you whispering to so-and-so, or someone saw so-and-so go into your office and close the door. The people who were watching will ask themselves, "What were they discussing? And why were they whispering? Were they talking about me? What do they know that I don't? Why won't they tell me?"

If you try to sneak out early to catch an earlier bus, remember that someone noticed that you left early. It doesn't make any difference that the person who saw you leave early is a co-worker or a manager. That you left early is what registered. That you just happened to have come to work early that day didn't register, primarily because the person who saw you leave early didn't see you come in early; and the reason that person didn't see you come in early was because you arrived in the office at 7:00 am, while that person didn't arrive until 9:15 am.

This isn't paranoia. It's a fact of life in the organization. At some point during the day, someone in the office sees what you are doing—or not doing. At some point during the day, someone in the office hears what you are saying. It's better to err on the side of caution, and to be as aware as possible of who is in the general vicinity.

CHAPTER 12

*c/c*

# Keep Your Salary to Yourself

---

*Familiarity does breed contempt. This becomes evident as soon as you hear about someone else's bonus.*

---

It happens every year. At some point during the year, the annual bonuses are announced. The announcement generally takes the form of an e-mail or a memo that gives percentages and dates. What isn't announced is how much each person is getting.

The formula works something like this. Each person is in a salary grade. The percentages that were announced are broad categories. Depending on your salary grade, you may get slightly more or slightly less than the announced percentage. Sometimes, there's a kicker for performance. So, instead of getting the announced 10 percent for your salary grade, you could get 12 or 13 percent, or even 8 percent. Whatever happens, do not tell anyone what you received. Letting people know is a perfect way to create enmity between you and your co-workers.

You would think that people who've worked for the company for ten or fifteen years would come to realize that the bonuses are gravy. In my case, the bonus is spent before it's even awarded. Anyway, I made the mistake of trusting in the integrity and maturity of a co-worker who immediately took umbrage at the difference between his bonus and my bonus. He didn't talk to me for a few weeks. Keep in mind that I didn't campaign for a better bonus, nor did I suck up to my manager. I received what I received, as I was told, as additional compensation for the work I was doing. That my co-worker didn't get as much as I did, or didn't get as much as he thought he deserved, is not my fault. So, why was he pissed off at me? Human nature is a funny thing.

Now, consider what happens when senior management tweaks the formula used to award bonuses. First, it's no longer called a bonus. It's now called "incentive compensation." Next, the awards are based on a completely arbitrary value system controlled by senior management. If senior management feels that you should get x percent, that's what you will get. You will not be rewarded for doing your job, but you will be rewarded for doing more than what is required. I can't say with certainty that those words appear anywhere, but that is precisely what we were told when our company changed the formula. This means that you can be the best widget maker in the company, and that your widgets are flawless, but you won't get the "incentive compensation," because all you do is make widgets.

Keep in mind that no one knows what anyone else is receiving. Trying to find out what someone else is getting becomes our raison d'être for the next several days. When we do find out what someone else is getting, and it doesn't measure up to our expectations—that is, the other person is getting more than we are, or the other person is getting more than we think he deserves—it makes for some very uncomfortable situations in the office.

Talk about vitriol! Intelligence and maturity go right out the window. We revert back to grammar school days, when opposing camps stood at opposite sides of the school yard and made scowling facial gestures toward each other in an attempt to incite a fight. Verbal swipes and cutting remarks become the norm for a few days. When sense returns, if it ever does, the normal routine resumes, but the scars remain. If you were one of the people who received more money, you will find that you have become branded by those who received less. By virtue of being better compensated, you give up your right to complain about the work environment. After all, you are better compensated, so you should be able to handle the stress, unlike the rest of us who, by virtue of being compensated less, have been effectively branded as less valuable.

Here is my suggestion for dealing with this situation. You may call it "rationalizing," but I call it "being pragmatic." I receive what I receive. If it fulfills the psychological contract with my employer—that is, if I received what I believe to be fair compensation in exchange for my services, regardless of what anyone else is receiving—then what anyone else receives is irrelevant. The fairness of the bonus lies in whether or not I believe it to be relevant to my performance. If my bonus is relevant to my performance, that's all that matters. That you received more than I received doesn't diminish what I received. That I received less than you received doesn't enhance what you received. Perhaps it's simply a matter of your ability to enhance your value to the organization in a way that I didn't think of doing for myself. In that case, you will eventually have to measure up to your own advertisement.

# CHAPTER 13

# Candor

> *Candor in a private forum could put your future in jeopardy. See chapters 2, 3, 4, 5, and 6.*

The fact that you are in a meeting with your fellow widget makers—just you, your co-workers, and your manager—does not insure you against retaliation for expressing an opinion that goes contrary to the official company position. Management insists that it does not want automatons among the rank and file. The staff should be creative, think outside the box, and take risks. That's all well and good, as long as what you are doing is consistent with the official company position.

If you make suggestions that your manager does not appreciate, or if you recommend a course of action that your manager doesn't like, regardless of how creative or forward-looking it may be, your suggestion or recommendation isn't going anywhere, and neither are you. Your manager and you may think along the same lines. That's good; but, it also means that you and your manager aren't going anywhere if you both agree that the official company position is wrong.

What if you and your manager do not think along the same lines? What if you and your manager keep butting heads over policies and procedures? You go along with the game plan only because you are told to go along, and you run the risk of becoming an automaton. You can't be a team player if you keep expressing contrary opinions, but you can't be creative if you keep coming up with ideas that everyone else has already expressed in one form or another. What do you do? Probably the most stress-relieving thing to do would be to stand up and say, "This whole thing is ridiculous, and I am not going along with it." This may be candor of the purest form, but it is likely to get you fired.

You have to decide whether or not it is appropriate to express a contrary opinion to the person whose job it is to get you to participate in senior management's plan. This is the person who will be writing your performance review; you are depending on him or her for a possible promotion. If you tell your manager that you don't agree with the plan, how can he or she recommend you for a promotion to the person whose plan you are criticizing? How far do you think you'll get if you criticize the plan face-to-face with the person who is trying to put the plan in motion? Remember human nature, the struggle between logic and emotion. What you are saying may make perfect sense, but if it gets your boss "pissed off," logic goes right out the window. Sometimes, being right can be the wrong choice.

New employees can get away with expressing contrary opinions. They haven't been around as long, and they haven't learned proper decorum. After a few years, you learn to recognize that senior management is not asking for your opinion. Yes, you are invited to express your opinion, but your opinion hasn't been specifically solicited.

The same holds true in the smaller private forums that don't involve most of the people in the organization. Contrary opinions reveal to management where the weak links are located. The weak links will be reinforced (you will be re-educated in some way), or the weak links will be cut out (you will be transferred or fired).

We generally think we should be honest and forthright when we have to talk about controversial issues. If we are in agreement on a topic, there is no controversy, and therefore, no need for candor. Candor in a private forum implies that there is controversy and, therefore, disagreement. The disagreement, not the candor, is most likely what will get you in trouble.

~~

# CHAPTER 14

# Speaking Up

*When you speak up at a forum, whether it is public or private, there will be consequences. This is particularly true if what you say goes counter to the prevailing management philosophy.*

This chapter has a slightly different thrust from that of the previous chapter. We're not talking about dealing with just management here. We're talking about dealing with co-workers who can make your life just as miserable as the manager can. You can score brownie points with management, but those points could put you at odds with your co-workers.

Here's a perfect example: A co-worker was trying to make a point about working from home, and she mentioned that she'd been working a number of hours on a task while she was at home. It came off sounding like, "Teacher, teacher, guess what I did yesterday!" Some of us took turns dumping on her at various times during the meeting, and from time to time over the next several weeks. Her statement didn't necessarily go against the prevailing management philosophy, but, it didn't seem to reinforce anyone's ideas, either. Privately, we thought that she was, to put it bluntly, a real kiss-ass. I don't know whether or not she ever realized what she said or how it sounded, but she never took the spotlight at another meeting after that incident.

People in the office become aware of what's expected of them, and they tend to cringe when a co-worker expresses an opinion that is not widely supported within the organization, even though they may agree privately with what is being said. The tendency is to reflect or to project the prevailing management philosophy, in case anyone is watching or listening. It is more of a reflex reaction, the way people cringe when they hear a loud noise.

If you say something publicly that goes counter to the prevailing management philosophy, you'll hear the collective groan permeate the room. The person running the meeting will attempt to maintain order by passing quickly through what you just said, and moving on to the next topic. Privately, your co-workers will heap "atta boys" on you. Publicly, your co-workers are trying to shield themselves from any fallout from what you said at the meeting, and they won't say anything praiseworthy about your statement. They will stare silently as you walk down the corridor, and may even whisper as you pass by. They are all thinking, "There but for the grace of God …."

What confuses people is the concept of freedom of speech. Yes, you have the right to say whatever you want to say, generally speaking, as long as it doesn't create a dangerous situation, such as yelling "fire" in a crowded theater. Being guaranteed the right to say what you want doesn't guarantee that there won't be any consequences. If you know that the people in charge will disagree with you, you have to expect that they will come at you, publicly or privately, for having expressed your opinion.

Don't be fooled into thinking that the manager agrees with you because he didn't argue the point. Sometimes, the appearance of gracious acceptance is nothing more than condescension. If you disagree with management, you are not a team player. The rest of the team will read the manager's reaction and will not want to make things worse by siding publicly with you. Their siding privately with you doesn't amount to much, because no one sees it or hears it. You stand out all by yourself, an easy target for anyone who wants to take a potshot at you.

CHAPTER 15

Ethics

*The importance of ethics varies inversely with
your position in the organization.*

There aren't too many "old timers" left in the organization, people who were involved in a debacle regarding the pay package of a certain chief executive officer. Whether or not he was entitled to the salary is not the issue. What is the issue is the elaborate choreography in which all the participants engaged.

We hold registered brokerage representatives (registered reps) to a particular standard: "Know your customer." Also, if the registered rep, or any employee of a member firm, engages in "conduct inconsistent with the just and equitable principles of trade," that person will be disciplined, fined, or barred from the industry for a specified period of time, or permanently, depending on the offense. If the broker's customer engages in questionable trading, and the broker has reason to believe that the trading is questionable, the broker is obligated to so advise the customer. If the customer trades on non-public information, and the broker has reason to believe that the customer is trading on non-public information, the broker has an obligation to notify his compliance department, or at the very least, his branch manager. If the broker himself engages in questionable trading, he is subject to various penalties.

Let's say I am on the Salary Committee of a particular company. (I'm not really, and I don't want to be.) The Salary Committee is responsible for determining, among other things, the salary of the CEO. That salary includes regular compensation and deferred compensation. For public companies, stock options may be part of the mix. In the same way that the broker has to know his customer, as a member of the Salary Committee, I should have to know the CEO. I should also have to know something about salaries, just as the securities broker has to know something about trading securities. If there is something that is questionable about the CEO, or if there is something that is questionable about the CEO's salary package, I am obliged to ask questions until I receive satisfactory answers. The satisfactory answer isn't, "Don't worry. The CEO knows what he's doing."

Let's face it. Saying "I didn't know" is unacceptable. In the same way that the broker is obligated to know his customer, as a member of the Salary Committee I should have known what I was approving when I approved the CEO's salary package. Similarly, the company executives and others who were responsible for facilitating this process share the responsibility to know. To the extent that they did know what was happening, and they facilitated what happened, it could be argued that they may have engaged in "conduct inconsistent ...," similar to the prohibition cited above for the registered representative. (No, I'm not a lawyer. The lawyers may argue that the logic of my comparison doesn't hold. Again, that's not the issue here. I'm using the comparison to illustrate a point.)

The members of the Salary Committee, and the company executives who assisted the Salary Committee, should be subject to the same sanctions, when sanctions are deemed suitable, as the broker who fails to take appropriate action regarding questionable trading by the client, or the broker who himself engages in questionable trading. Just as the broker is responsible for alerting his branch manager or compliance department about questionable trading, the members of the Salary Committee and the company executives who were assisting the Salary Committee are responsible for alerting— the CEO? There you have your ethics dilemma. (In this instance, the CEO is also the Chairman of the Board.)

In my company, people were told that everyone would be ranked according to their performance; that meant that someone would come out at the top and someone would come out at the bottom. The fact that more than one person was a top performer was irrelevant. They couldn't all be rated "good." Someone would have to be rated "bad," even if that person's performance was good. (Those sucking sounds that you hear are caused by the air seeping through the spaces between people's lips and managers' asses, a result of people trying to find a way to supplement their performance in order to be rated "good.") It would seem to me to be a question of ethics to rate someone as "needs improvement" simply because someone had to be at the bottom, even if that person didn't deserve to be rated "needs improvement." Similarly, it would be a question of ethics to rate someone as "outstanding" simply because someone had to be at the top, even if that person was in no way outstanding.

Refusing to recognize a job done well, even if it's the same job that the person has been doing for several years, says something about the manager who is writing the performance review, and it speaks volumes about the executive who instituted the policy.

There's a saying in Brooklyn that you've got to do the right thing. Some of the executives and managers in the company have to learn to do the right thing by their subordinates.

It just feels as though the higher up you get in the organization, the more you are forced to rationalize behavior that appears unethical to people lower in the organizational hierarchy. Maybe it's because we're looking up at the tower instead of looking down from the top of the tower. When you're that high up, the things at the bottom look miniscule, just as the things at the top look when you're staring up from the bottom. To me, ethics is the antivert that will keep you from getting dizzy when you're that high up and in danger of falling over the railing.

CHAPTER 16

*m*

# The Purpose of Meetings

---

*The purpose of department/division meetings is
to announce to the staff what has already been
decided. See chapters 4, 13, and 14.*

---

"Thank you all for coming. I scheduled this meeting so that
we would have the opportunity to discuss what's been going
on during these hectic times. I just want you all to know
blah blah blah blah ..." This is generally how most of the
division meetings proceed; perhaps not these exact words,
and certainly not the blah blah blah part, although the blah
blah blah part is pretty much what people hear. Anything that
senior management "discusses" at a division meeting is not
open to discussion. If someone in the audience asks a question
or offers a comment, that person is met with polite dismissal,
or the comment is itself offered up for comment.

It's rare that any announcement at these meetings is really an
announcement. The meetings at the water cooler are a better
source of information than any formal announcement at a
division meeting. What the division meetings (or the department
meetings, or the general company meetings, which staff are invited

to attend via remote access from the PC) do is confirm what has been rumored during the preceding weeks. Maybe at some level in the organization these meetings serve a real purpose and aren't organized just to have something to include in a weekly report.

Information flows through any organization by various means. If promotions are announced, the people who are being promoted have already told some of their friends. If procedural changes are being announced, the changes have already been discussed at the staff level to give advance notice to the people whose jobs are affected. If there are major policy changes, and these changes have been the subject of newspaper articles, you are led to believe that the purpose of the meeting is to set the record straight, or to clarify a misconception, or to correct a misstatement in the press. In fact, the major policy change is already in the news, and the affected parties were already advised, either formally or informally, about the change.

There are those rare occasions when the staff is advised about policy changes before any public announcement was made, or when the staff is advised or warned about procedural changes before the changes are formally put in place. The nature of the businesses of the companies for which I worked practically required that the staff be notified, whether formally or informally, that changes were coming down the pike. We'd know that a procedure would change, or that a new policy was being enforced, before the formal announcement was made. Yet, management continues to try to make the announcements sound like a revelation. Stop insulting our intelligence!

There may be some legitimacy to calling division or department meetings to "discuss" recent events or policy changes. It gives senior management the opportunity to say it once in a forum where the staff can hear it directly from the source. There is no opportunity to offer criticism, positive or negative, or to offer an alternative position, for those have already been considered by the senior executives long before the division or department meeting was even planned.

I don't believe that a senior executive would convene a general staff meeting to announce important policy changes and then invite comments to help him decide whether or not to move forward with those changes. It's more likely that the decision to move forward was made long before the staff meeting was convened, as I suggested earlier. If we go into those meetings understanding how the process works, and if we recognize those meetings for what they are and not what we hope they will be, we will not be disappointed. Instead of attending the meeting believing it will be a waste of time because we won't learn anything new, we should use the meeting as an opportunity to get a read on the real impact of what's being discussed or announced. We should notice:

- The seating arrangement, and who follows whom in the speaking order
- How introductions are made and accepted, and where the speaker's eyes are looking when he or she is speaking
- Whether or not the speaker uses a lot of "ums" and "ahs," or if the speaker's voice changes in any way
- Whether or not the speaker appears agitated when responding to a specific question or comment, and who is asking the question or making the comment

Herein lies the value of these division/department meetings— not in the subject matter but in the subtleties and nuances of body language, speech cadence and inflection, and the information that these things convey.

# Accentuating the Negative

*You can do a thousand or more things right that people may remember; but, people will always recall the things you did wrong.*

Once I made the ghastly mistake of sending out an e-mail to everyone in the division by inadvertently clicking on "Respond to All." The topic of the e-mail set a few people off, including the senior division executive. I ended up apologizing to the senior executive in an attempt to head off his taking it out on the department manager and on my supervisor. I did not apologize for what I said, but I apologized for using the wrong forum to express my opinion. I waited for the dust to settle. It never did. Though the jokes continued years after the incident occurred, they stopped being funny about five minutes after it happened.

What about all the things I did right? OK, I can't exactly recite for you all the details of each occurrence. The point is that I don't hear anyone reminding me of what I did that was right. You're thinking, "Maybe it's because you didn't do too many things that were right." Maybe it's human nature to keep count of the errors, to avoid too many entries in the "minus" column. As a result, we don't keep an accurate count of all the entries in the "plus" column.

The same concept holds true when we assess the merits of a co-worker. Remember, we are at the same time allies and adversaries. While we may be willing to come to the aid of a co-worker, are we prepared to extol his virtues to the higher-ups? Yes, but not to the extent of making him look better than we do.

A former business acquaintance gave me some good advice. He said, "Always take the job seriously, but never take yourself seriously." In my office, greetings among co-workers sometimes take the form of a Don Rickles compliment. It's all in fun and meant to keep things loose. I believe that at my level in the organization, this looseness makes for better communication. We try not to take ourselves too seriously, as my former business acquaintance recommended to me.

The problem is that the funny comments are made so often and so routinely that I start wondering whether or not the person making the comments (myself included) really feels that way. The comments always focus on something negative, or something that is not so positive. It is in this vein that people regularly talk about each other's mistakes and mishaps. I believe that this may contribute to our tendency to recall mistakes and overlook successes, the tendency always to remember what we did wrong, and only occasionally recollect something that we did right.

# CHAPTER 18

Special Committees and Task Forces

*The purpose of a special committee or a task force is to reinforce management's philosophy, or to facilitate implementation of management's agenda. See chapter 16.*

Were you ever invited to become part of a "special committee" to develop a new procedure, or to join a "task force" to examine current procedures, with the idea of revising them in light of current regulations and practices? The group consists of staff-level employees, one or two supervisors, and maybe a mid-level officer, or even a senior-level officer in the division. A member of the group, usually a supervisor or an officer, will be the chairman who sets the tone and focus of the group. The group's mission will be to come up with a revised procedure to address issues raised by x, or to develop a new procedure to address y.

That a new procedure or a revised procedure will have to be developed has already been determined. As a member of the committee, you may offer an opinion that a revised procedure isn't needed, or that a new procedure won't add anything that isn't already being addressed. That is irrelevant. The committee or the task force must come up with something to present to senior management.

Your logical explanation for why nothing needs to be revised or added will never be heard by anyone outside of the group. Management, or someone who is influencing management, has decided that something has to be done; and the committee or the task force is the vehicle by which that something will be developed. The chairman of the committee, or the head of the task force, will deliver that something to management. It will be done. You are member of the committee. You bear some of the responsibility for failure (generally). You may share the kudos for success.

The whole idea of these groups is to convey legitimacy to whatever will be proposed; whatever will be proposed has already been determined, and its implementation has already been decided. It's just a matter of when it will become part of the procedure, not if it will become part of the procedure.

Your participation in the group is not predicated on your expertise in the field, or on your knowledge of the subject, although your expertise in the field will lend legitimacy to the proposal and your knowledge of the subject will lend credence to the plan. You are chosen to become part of the group for appearances only. That way, senior management can proudly proclaim that a special committee composed of an array of staff members with experience in the field came up with the proposals to respond to the concerns raised by x or y. The reality is that senior management has already decided what will happen.

One group had to develop a new series of procedures to deal with different analytical protocols as a result of a merger. The protocols of the two companies were so disparate that the existing procedures couldn't adequately address the issues raised by the protocols that were used by the company that was acquired. There wasn't much of a choice. Senior management had already decided that the protocols would be integrated; the group had to come up with a way of adequately integrating the protocols that would satisfy the regulators.

The entire effort was a major disaster, in my opinion. The databases were never integrated, and they couldn't be, due to their different origins. Working with these different protocols became the norm rather than the exception. You'd think that someone in the organization would have addressed these concerns before the merger was completed. Where was the special committee that was supposed to work on this project? What happened to the task force that was supposed to come up with a unified approach to the analysis?

What happened, in this instance, was that the differences and disparities became non-issues because senior management determined that nothing would get in the way of the merger's occurring according to the established timetable. Some would argue that there were legal impediments to sharing information prior to completion of the merger. Logic should have trumped legality in this instance, and someone should have taken the reins in organizing a task force to address the differences between the analytical protocols.

There was no need to reinforce management's philosophy, or to facilitate implementation of an agenda. The philosophy was not an issue; the agenda was a fait accompli. What this showed was that if you see something on the horizon, whether or not it may actually occur, you have to address it so that if committee assignments are announced, you'll be ready to present to senior management the plan that they want.

That these committee assignments weren't formally part of the overall plan was irrelevant. If they weren't part of the overall plan, the fact that you volunteered showed that you were being proactive in forming the committees. It they were part of the overall plan, you showed that you were a team player in opting to become a member. The purpose of the creation of special committee or a task force was to formulate what was already decided.

# CHAPTER 19

The Company's Goals are Your Goals

*If it's important to the person in charge, it's important to you. That it doesn't make any sense is irrelevant. See chapter 7.*

I've always said, "Don't tell me what without telling me why." Implicit in that statement is that I need to understand why you are doing what you are doing before I will agree to go along. This makes sense outside the company. Inside the company, such logic does not exist. The division executive has put forth his agenda for what he expects the division to accomplish this year. The expectation is that you will do what must be done in order to accomplish those objectives. Why he wants those things done is a separate issue. All you need to know is that the division executive wants what he wants. There's a deadline imposed, and we have to meet that deadline.

You run into problems when you start questioning management's logic. You have to remember that the objectives of the senior executive are not necessarily born out of the same concerns that you have at your level of the organization. He's being dumped on by the CEO. He, in turn, dumps on the department manager, who dumps on the supervisor, who dumps on you. At each level the concerns are different, but driven by the same survival instinct. My concern is doing my job well, being adequately recognized for my accomplishments, and being appropriately compensated for my output. That is probably the same concern at each level of the organization. What it involves at higher levels differs from what it involves at lower levels.

The logic that drives a management decision is not so clearly discernable to the rank and file. If you ask why, you will be told why. If you don't understand the explanation, you will be given a more detailed explanation. If you don't agree, you are told that it's OK to disagree, but you still have to go along with the game plan. If you persist in your questioning, you are not a team player. (Remember that in the company, perception is reality.)

Now you have a problem, and the problem will cause stress. The problem is that you have to do something that doesn't make any sense to you, for reasons with which you don't agree, and you will be evaluated on how well you accomplish your mission. The temptation is to do the job halfheartedly, but that would lead to an even bigger mistake. You begin to believe your own perception, which is that what you are being told to do doesn't make any sense, and therefore, no one will really expect you to do anything. So, you do nothing with the expectation that there will be no reprisals. Wrong!

The best antidote for this malaise is simply to accept management's pronouncement of what is to be accomplished. Ignore the explanation that you were given, and do what must be done because that's what management wants. The logic that drives what you do at your level can be summed up with these words: "Because that's the way management wants it done."

Keep in mind that there is still plenty of room for creativity. Although the senior executive has given the order, he probably left it up to the department managers and supervisors to determine how to carry out his order. This is where you focus your energy, not on what he told the staff to do, but on how you will get the job done.

Don't stop to think about why you perform any specific task. Look at the totality of the accomplishment. You are managing to produce output that is satisfactory to the senior executive, which makes life for the department manager a bit easier, and so on down the line. Once you stop to analyze the logic of what you do, you will develop an intellectual short circuit. You will start questioning the logic of every task that you perform throughout the day. Eventually, you will question the logic of the company's existence. At that point, you are able to accomplish nothing because of your inability to motivate yourself. When logic fails to motivate you, your survival instincts should take over. This is just one situation in which you don't want to do nothing.

# CHAPTER 20

# Your Manager Is Not Your Friend

---

*Your manager is your manager, first and
foremost. See chapter 3.*

---

The manager's job is to get you to do your job. In order to do
that, your manager will use different methods that can range
from friendly persuasion to outright force. In the organization,
outright force takes on a new dimension. In forcing you to do
your job, your manager may not take a combative stance, but
merely invoke sanctions against you, such as a lower merit
increase. You can generally tell when you are being forced to do
something. It's when your manager assumes a friendly posture
that you have to ask yourself, "What does she really want"?

As I said earlier, don't confuse someone who is friendly with
someone who is a friend. Friends are often friendly, but
people who are friendly aren't always being your friends. Your
manager has a job to do, and you have a job to do. If you
aren't motivated, your manager's job is to motivate you. Your
manager will draw from her skills database and come up with
a way to motivate you. It can be as simple as asking you in a

nice way, or as obvious as reading you the riot act. Either you are motivated to act, or you suffer the consequences.

Now this doesn't mean that you can't commiserate with your manager, or that you should refrain from engaging in social banter. It means that you have to remember your place in the food chain, and that you are valuable to the organization to the extent that you are able to support your manager. That is, your manager will value your services more if you can supplement or complement her capabilities. It can be something as simple as getting the correspondence prepared for her signature before being asked for it instead of waiting for her to tell you to prepare the correspondence for her signature.

Maybe you're creative when it comes to editing your own memos. Your manager will make corrections, but you don't have to follow the corrections verbatim as long as you don't change the meaning of what she intended to write. (You'd be amazed at how many memos and letters I write are edited by my manager and the department manager. When I receive the marked copies, I edit the edits to conform to my writing style while still maintaining the thrust of the corrected versions of the memo or the letter.) Perhaps you are able to anticipate the comments that the department manager will make and write the memo according to her style. Either way, you are supporting management, and your services are valued accordingly. Your manager is happy and the staff is happy, but your manager is still your manager, regardless of how calm she may appear, or how friendly her demeanor may be.

Just as you have to accept your manager's quirky habits or succumb to her management style in order to survive, your manager will learn to accept your pain-in-the-ass attitude as long as you make a positive contribution to the organization. Everyone gets along if everyone cooperates with each other to the extent necessary to facilitate survival. You can be friendly with your manager, but being friends with your manager isn't the best course to follow. You've got to maintain that distance that will help to keep things in focus. Get too close, and things get blurry. Stay far enough away, and your vision stays in focus. Find that median distance and stay there. It'll be best for everyone involved.

The relationship that you have with your manager has obvious consequences, not the least of which is how she will assess your contribution to the organization during performance appraisal time. It's OK to argue from time to time as long as neither of you becomes argumentative, with the result that the argument turns into a fight. You have to maintain your objectivity as an employee, see the argument for what it is, and go along with the game plan. You may be right, but rank in the organization always trumps logic.

If your manager happens to be your friend, your opposing point of view forces her to choose job over friendship, if only for that situation. Will either of you be sensible enough to realize that she is trying to be a manager, and that you are the employee? Actually, both of you are employees, but, she is higher up on the totem pole than you are. One of you will have to yield the point of the argument, and your manager can't lose face; it would weaken her ability to manage.

Some managers are intelligent enough to be able to assess how capable an employee is based on how the employee argues his point. It may simply be that the manager is challenging you to see how you'll react. If you melt down, and transition from arguing to fighting, you lose. The bottom line? Your manager is your manager. She will try to help you when necessary, but, if you don't fulfill your part of the bargain, the next time around—there won't be a next time around.

# CHAPTER 21

Trust

---

*The quality of life in the organization varies directly with the level of trust between you and your co-workers/managers.*

---

Do not confuse trust with friendship. Friendship is not necessary for you to survive within the organization, but trust is essential. The quality of life in the organization varies directly with the level of trust between you and your co-workers/managers.

How much of your strength and vitality is wasted by constantly and continually looking over your shoulder in an effort to protect yourself from actions and retaliations that may never happen, or that happen all too frequently? You spend most of your time trying to protect yourself from real or imagined occurrences because you don't trust the people with whom you work.

Maybe there was something that happened that taught you that you cannot trust your co-workers. It sucks the life out of you. You have to go to a place of business five days a week, if not more, and spend your time with people who are just waiting for you to falter, or who would cause you to falter, just to have the advantage at performance review time. Each of us has limited physical and mental resources that we dedicate to doing our jobs while the rest of our lives operate on autopilot. In a situation where you have to watch your back all the time, you end up straining those limited resources just so that you can do what you're paid to do.

I'm not suggesting that every place of business has to turn into a lovefest. You don't have to like the people with whom you work, but you have to be able to trust them. You have to know where you stand with them so that you know what you can or cannot accomplish (or can/cannot get away with, depending on your frame of reference). Trust is essential in order for you to survive within the organization.

You have to be able to depend on your co-workers to do their jobs so that you can do your job. Friendship may help in the short run, but friendships have their own downside that can wreak havoc when it comes to making decisions and taking actions that result in one of you getting rapped on the knuckles. The relationships that you develop with your co-workers probably contribute as much to your job satisfaction as do your own accomplishments. You can be a stellar performer, but if you find yourself not interacting regularly with your co-workers, I suggest that you are missing out on a very important part of the job: building a network.

It's important to build a network of relationships as a safety net just in case something bad happens on the job and you need backup. You need people on whom you can depend, to bail you out of a jam, or at the very least, offer moral support. You shouldn't have to think twice about approaching a co-worker, especially one who is doing the same job as you are, to ask for his perspective on a problem you're having with a client, or to get ideas on how to solve a problem with some analysis you have to perform.

The same goes for the relationship that you have with your manager. If you have to try to figure out what his agenda is (we all have agendas, remember?) because you don't trust him, it's time to look for another position where you don't have to deal with him. He may have different goals and aspirations, but his agenda and your agenda, as far as the job is concerned, should be approximately the same.

Think about this for a minute. You really like what you do for a living. The work is challenging; it changes almost every day, with no two problems presenting the same fact pattern. But you really can't stand some of the people with whom you work. You find yourself making minor changes to your work habits just so you don't have to deal with the people you don't like. I can tell you from experience that eventually you will have to deal with one or more of those people; you will need their expertise on a problem you have to solve.

You can't have misgivings about everyone in the office. If that's your situation, get out now while you still have your sanity. Find another position in the company. If that isn't possible, find another position at another company. You need to work in an environment that is conducive to productivity. Of course, sometimes you have to make that environment for yourself, and having co-workers and managers on whom you can rely is a major part of that environment.

What happens if the people you don't trust are at or near the top of the corporate hierarchy? Here is where you have to be able to rely on your manager, assuming that your manager isn't the senior executive you don't trust.

One of your manager's tasks is to interpret the directives of senior management in a way that will get you to go along with the game plan. Sometimes it's just a matter of saying that it has to be done because senior management wants it done; and there isn't any logic involved. If your immediate supervisor is adept at conveying that message to you, you owe it to her to follow the orders, if only because of her honesty. Otherwise, you have a decision to make.

You have to decide whether or not you're going to buy into whatever management is selling. If you find that your logic is being short-circuited when you try to comply with what senior management wants, you must reconstruct your logic to be in sync with management's directives, or you must reconfigure your agenda in a way that enables you to maintain your sense of balance without undermining management's agenda. It would be much easier if you could just *trust* the judgment of your manager.

# Chapter 22

# You Are Not Indispensible

*Everyone and everything is expendable.*

The organization is driven by motive and objective. The motive and objective are instilled by senior management and the board of directors. People are placed in key positions in the organization to facilitate achieving the objective and to inspire the staff to do the same. When the people in those key positions stop delivering, they are replaced. The replacement is sometimes cloaked in the veil of "reassignment" or "early retirement," but be assured that they are being replaced because they are no longer useful to the organization in achieving its objective.

People throughout the organization will be put in harm's way, in a manner of speaking, if it leads to successful achievement of the corporate objective. Think of the movie scene where the troops are facing the enemy in a major battle. The officer in charge sends one or more soldiers out on a special mission, knowing that some may not return. There's also the scene where the officer in charge leaves a group of soldiers to draw fire so that the rest of the platoon can engage the enemy at a different location. In each example, someone has decided that there are people whose lives are expendable for the greater good. Who is expendable, and for what purpose, are separate issues. There are one or more people in charge who decide every day that people will be transferred or dismissed because their presence no longer serves the corporate objective.

It used to be that the writing would be on the wall way before you got your pink slip. Well, that doesn't happen anymore. If someone wants you out, you're out, without any warning, and without the benefit of the writing on the wall that would have given you a chance to find another position before the ax came down.

It happened in my company. I could not prove it, but I personally knew of at least one person who was let go in the name of downsizing. He insisted that there was no warning. He was called into the manager's office in the afternoon and told that it was his last day. He was replaced with someone younger and more to the manager's liking. The new employee's youth and the manager's preference may or may not have been the motives. Whether they were the reason or not, my former co-worker was out of a job after nineteen years with the company. There was no chance to relocate to another department and no opportunity for a lateral move, or even a demotion.

This doesn't only apply to people. Hundreds, if not thousands, of pounds of paper products, in the form of old stationery, excess inventory of three-ring binders, manila folders, and things of that nature, get thrown out each year instead of being recycled or reused in some way. Of course, one wonders why the supplies were ordered in the first place.

There's a photocopy machine in the office now that malfunctions regularly, at least three or four times a month. The malfunction results in hundreds of pages of unusable photocopies being discarded. We waste the paper, but will not replace the photocopy machine. You'd think that the photocopy machine was more expendable than the paper, given the apparently poor quality of the machine. Again, someone has decided to the contrary for some arbitrary reason that defies logic.

The expending of people and things by the organization is a matter of corporate survival. Corporations are separate entities in the eyes of the law. These entities struggle to survive, much as living, breathing human beings do. People have been known to jettison unwanted family members because the cost of maintenance was too great. Think divorce and child abandonment. The organization is doing the same thing, but society doesn't always frown upon it; it's legal and necessary in the eyes of management and the board of directors. People discard furniture in order to keep with the current trends, and not because the furniture is old and cannot be repaired. Clothing is thrown out or donated because it's yesterday's style, and not necessarily because it is worn or it doesn't fit anymore. It seems to me that companies treat staff like old furniture or clothing, at least the ones that management no longer wants on the payroll.

# CHAPTER 23

# Have a Backup Plan

*You should always have a Plan B just in case
Plan A doesn't work.*

What will you do if your original plan didn't work out the way you planned? Don't say, "I don't know." That means that you didn't plan well enough, look far enough, or think long enough. However long you thought it would take to do what you wanted to do, figure at least twice as long. We can only control what we do, and we can only plan what we want to do. We can't possibly know what everyone has planned; therefore, we can't possibly know how our plan will turn out. Remember what I said about people's agendas.

One way of looking at this problem is that you have to come up with alternative plans equal to the number of people you have to deal with every day. If you typically deal with ten or fifteen people, you have to have ten or fifteen alternatives available, depending on how these other people will react to what you are doing, and to what extent they can impact your plan. If out of those ten or fifteen people, only two or three can make or break your career, you really only have to worry about those two or three people, and you have to have two or three alternatives. That's if you want to play the game. If you don't want to play the game, you have to be ready to react to the whim of the person who runs the show. Your plan may end up in the toilet if the person in charge has other ideas.

Try this perspective. You know what you want to do. The first action you take will elicit a reaction. Now you have to assess that reaction and formulate your next step. That next step will elicit a reaction. Now you have to assess that reaction and formulate your next step. The process continues for every action that you take. You can guess as to the reactions of others, but you can't possibly know in advance how the people in charge will react.

You also have to consider the reactions of your immediate supervisor and your co-workers. Your immediate supervisor is the department manager's information filter, unless you have a direct line to the department manager. Your co-workers, to the extent that they can influence your supervisor or the department manager, will impact every step in your plan, too. So what do you do? You can't fall victim to paralysis by analysis. You make a plan, and you make a backup plan. If the plan doesn't work, or if it starts to fall apart, you resort to your alternative. If the alternative doesn't work, or if it also falls apart, you develop another alternative, and so the process continues.

You don't want to find yourself in a situation where you are saying, "I didn't think that would happen." There's a difference between thinking that something will not happen, and thinking that something is not likely to happen. If you think that something will not happen, you ignore it and move on to the next item. If you think that something is not likely to happen, you have to allow for the possibility that it may happen. You've decided to play the odds.

You evaluate your plan and the alternative, and you determine, or guess, as to the possible reactions or outcomes. You assign probabilities (sounds like a math class) to each outcome, and you address the outcomes with the greatest probability of occurring. Still, you must never lose sight of those outcomes that are less likely to happen. That they are less likely to happen doesn't mean that they won't happen. Of course, you have to consider the costs in terms of time and effort that you put into assessing all of the possible outcomes.

At some point, you will draw the line and say that these are the possible outcomes that you will address, and you will not bother with the others because the likelihood of occurrence for those outcomes doesn't warrant any additional input or effort. It's OK to do that as long as you recognize the risk of drawing the line in the wrong place: that you will have ignored some alternatives that you should have considered when you first developed your plan.

This is difficult to do on a daily basis. So you have to develop a long-term perspective. Don't try to micromanage everything every day. Keep your eyes and ears open and your mouth shut. Listen to what people are saying. Watch what they are doing. Determine as best you can the message that is being communicated, not just what is actually being said. Understand the position that each person occupies, in terms of how they interact with management and their peers. That will give you a hint as to their motives, if not the message to which they are responding. Try to recognize the truism that is being communicated within the organization. That truism is the reality that you must address in formulating your plans.

# CHAPTER 24

## Corporate Announcements

---

*In true Orwellian fashion, the corporate announcements mean whatever management wants them to mean.*

---

I've collected a few excerpts from memos, e-mails, and various other items that were circulated among the staff at a company.

- "High potential staff attended the Introductory Project Management Techniques and Team Leadership Skills program."

What exactly is "high potential staff"? What if you weren't included in the group? Does that mean you are "low potential staff"? As an aside, most of the people who attended the program are no longer with the company. What does that say about high potential staff? More to the point, what does that say about the person who wrote the memo that contained the now infamous phrasing?

- "We expect that no employee will knowingly place himself or herself in a position that would have the appearance of being, or could be construed to be, in conflict with the interests of [the company]."

What exactly are the interests of the company, aside from the obvious ones? Suddenly, the company takes an interest in something, and because I put myself in a position that conflicts with that interest before the company took an interest in it, I am in deep doo-doo? We have to look beyond the obvious and consider the interests or *potential interests* of the company.

- "At all times when acting on behalf of [the company], all employees are expected to act in the interest of [the company]."

Does this mean that if an employee is not acting on behalf of the company, he can act in a manner that conflicts with the interests of the company?

- "Because each such situation may involve special circumstances, [the company] will judge each on its own merits."

Does this mean that the company will decide on an ad hoc basis what constitutes a conflict and what doesn't? If you weren't acting on behalf of the company, but what you were doing conflicted with the interests of the company, where does that fit in the conflicts of interest policy? Wherever the company says it fits.

One of my former employers had a policy that stated essentially that an employee was not permitted to own certain securities in accounts in his name or in accounts over which he had influence. Since I didn't know what "influence" meant, I asked our ethics officer. The question involved my mother's brokerage account. My mother would ask my brothers, my sister, and me whether or not she should buy/sell what her broker was recommending. According to the ethics officer, I had influence over my mother's account and therefore, the restrictions that applied to me also applied to her. That meant that my mother was required to dispose of certain stocks that I as an employee was not permitted to own.

Almost everyone in my department chided me for asking the question. I questioned the interpretation of the policy. That no one else seemed to have the same questions that I had was totally irrelevant. As it turned out, the company insisted that my mother dispose of several stocks that she refused to sell. That forced me to get my mother to sign a letter stating that she would no longer be asking me for advice. I also had to provide a signed statement that I would no longer be giving my mother advice on her account. My co-workers figured that having influence meant being named as a co-owner of the account, or as having discretionary authority over the account, neither of which applied to me and my mother.

As I see it, the company policies are meant to provide a framework within which all employees are expected to act. The policies set limits, provide guidance, and establish rewards and penalties, among other things. If an act or a circumstance doesn't fit neatly within any of the categories identified in the policies, management must decide how that particular circumstance fits, and how to deal with it.

What the company does not do is document each of these decisions in order to establish precedent for the next occurrence. The reason the company does not document these decisions, in my opinion, is that management doesn't want to create or establish a precedent. We are given the usual rhetoric about not being tied to the past, moving forward, and being creative in meeting new challenges, blah blah blah. It's all in how you frame the issue. Once the issue is framed, the response is obvious. Frame it differently, and you get a different response. None of this is documented anywhere, so there's no proof. The policy today has no bearing on the policy tomorrow.

CHAPTER 25

*~m~*

# Make the Best of the Situation

---

*You cannot make a silk purse from a sow's ear;*
*but, you may be able to find new ways to use*
*a sow's ear*

---

In any organization, you have three choices. You can work with the circumstance you're handed, you can work around the circumstance you're handed, or you can leave. I don't think there's anything wrong with leaving, but it's more of a challenge and more rewarding if you can find a way to survive within the organization.

Some of my co-workers have become quite adept at working around people and situations that prevent them from performing their assigned tasks. Others have become proficient at working with people and circumstances that would test the patience of Job. These employees are showing the kind of creativity that management keeps telling us we should show in addressing challenges, and they are surviving in the new environment.

Come to think of it, dealing with senior management

forces department managers and supervisors to be creative in responding to management's demands. That creativity, in some departments, has become an end in itself. Procedures are sometimes developed on the fly. This is a problem since there are procedures that address how to develop new procedures, and there are procedures to be followed in order to get the new procedures approved. That these department managers and their staffs are able to get anything done within the framework established by senior management is a testament to their creativity. They have found a new way to use a sow's ear.

A popular misconception is that if something isn't very good to start with, you can't do much to improve it. I submit that my co-workers—the department managers and staff referenced above—have done an excellent job of taking something that wasn't very good and improving it.

They were asked to produce a silk purse—the output requested by senior management. They started out with a sow's ear—the input thrown together as a result of conflicting procedures. They used their creativity to meet the objectives.

We sometimes must avoid complaining about the circumstances, even if the circumstances warrant the complaints. As I said before, we should try to deal with the circumstances as given. The challenge is to succeed in spite of the situation. If we can make the silk purses from the sow's ears, that is, if we can make the improvements that we need in order to meet the company's objectives, that's what has to be done in order for us to survive in the organization.

# Epilogue

*Some Miscellaneous Observations*

We can't control what others do. We can only control what we do. We can't force the company to bend to our way of thinking. Remember what I said earlier about agendas. Survival in the organization means marrying one's goals and aspirations to those of the organization. Otherwise, we're just hanging on for the ride, and we'll get flung off at the first sharp turn or speed bump.

If the supervisor is a bonehead, you don't have to be one, too. You can still maintain your identity; just do it in a way that makes the supervisor think that he's in control, and that you're doing his bidding. Of course, if he's on senior management's hit list, which isn't too farfetched if he's a bonehead, you'll have to engage in some fancy footwork in order to keep from being dragged down with him while still convincing him that you're on his team. That could mean that at some point you'll have to let everyone know that you intend to survive with all your body parts intact, meaning that you'll have to cut ties with your supervisor.

If you've done your job, if you've managed to accomplish what senior management wanted to accomplish despite what your supervisor has been doing, cutting ties with your supervisor will come naturally. You've been doing the work all along. You've been producing the reports to which he attached his name, and you've been cushioning his fall every time he stumbled. Just take a step back the next time he stumbles. He will fall, and this time you will not bear any strain caused by his injuries.

Fighting windmills isn't so hard when others are fighting windmills with you. When you're out there by yourself, and Sancho Panza isn't around to help you, it's a different story. You have to decide whether or not the benefit, if there is one, is worth the cost. Don't be altruistic. Your co-workers, once they become your former co-workers, won't think twice about you when you're gone. They have their own agendas to which they must attend. Instead of fighting the imaginary enemy by yourself, try to find the point where your agenda intersects with your co-workers' agendas, and enlist their support for a common cause.

Learn to appreciate tacit recognition. We all have egos to protect, and the senior manager will rarely, if ever, proclaim to the staff that he was wrong. If the senior manager has been pushing for X while you've been recommending Y, rather than admit that you may be right and he may be wrong, the manager may quietly retreat from X and let Y happen. You won't get any kudos for it; but, anyone who's been paying attention will know what happened and why. If you were expecting public recognition for your contribution and didn't get it, that's the risk you took. If public recognition was the only reason you undertook the project, then that is your mistake. You have to move on, either within the organization or with another organization.

You don't have to fight every fight. You should choose your battles, and make sure that they are your battles and not someone else's. Some of the things you may want to consider are:

- Is there a reward for the risk you are taking?
- What are your chances of seeing that reward?
- Do you even want the reward?
- Are you taking all the risk while someone else is reaping the reward?

Use these as guidelines for deciding whether you want to join the fray.

If you stay on the merry-go-round long enough, everything starts to look blurry. You may get used to going in circles and completely forget about reaching for the brass ring. If the job is nothing more than a paycheck, find something else to help you self-actualize.

The competition isn't going to get any easier, and the competitors will probably be getting younger as you grow older. There's no shame in hopping off the merry-go-round and opting for something less circuitous. If you're good at what you do, there's no need to compete. The newcomers will be competing against you, and you should let them. Stay focused. The newcomer may win, but that doesn't mean that you automatically lose, unless you made the job your life's goal.

There is a saying that's appropriate here. It's somewhat raunchy, so I'll try to tone it down a little: Even some turds float. People who don't have talent, or who aren't as talented as you are, may make their way up the organizational ladder. Eventually, someone will notice the aroma, and will trace it to its source. Can you say "flush"? Consider whether or not you believe that you are being adequately compensated, regardless of what others in the organization are earning. If the answer is "yes," it shouldn't make any difference that someone else got the promotion. If you are at that level where such things matter, then you either develop a survival strategy (continue to fight), or you try to retreat with dignity (find another job).

Be very careful about developing an "attitude." Don't isolate yourself. Networking is often as important as working, and you can't network in a vacuum. Focus on the big picture. That is, try to look beyond your immediate circumstance. Consider all the "what ifs" and factor them into your decision whether or not to play the game.

I never really learned how to play the game. Now that I'm no longer a player, assuming that I was ever a "player," I've had time to consider all aspects of the job. I now realize the necessity of going along with the game plan. I've often wondered, however, whether or not it's possible to buy into the premise without compromising one's principles.

My experiences on Wall Street have shaped my outlook. In my current endeavors, I'm drawing on those experiences in an effort to avoid making the same mistakes. I've come to understand that a certain amount of compromise is necessary. If one's focus is on winning (assuming that one is an active player in the game), compromise is inevitable. I was never able to compromise without feeling guilty. There's no room on Wall Street for people who feel guilty about compromise.

I didn't self-destruct. I left the game. Did I lose? No, I survived. I won!

www.ingramcontent.com/pod-product-compliance
Lightning Source LLC
Chambersburg PA
CBHW030410290526
45785CB00004B/1952